P9-CRO-712

The Question & Answer Book

AMAZING WORLD OF ANIMALS

AMAZING WORLD OF ANIMALS

By Lawrence Jefferies
Illustrated by Tony D'Adamo

Troll Associates

Library of Congress Cataloging in Publication Data

Jefferies, Lawrence.
    Amazing world of animals.

    (The Question and answer book)
    Summary: Questions and answers provide a wide range
of basic information about animals, including such topics
as classification, migration, hibernation, and habitats.
        1. Animals—Miscellanea—Juvenile literature.
[1. Animals.   2. Questions and answers]   I. D'Adamo,
Anthony, ill.   II. Title.   III. Series: Question and
answer book (Troll Associates)
QL49.J4   1983   591   82-20061
ISBN 0-89375-898-1
ISBN 0-89375-899-X (pbk.)

Copyright © 1983 by Troll Associates, Mahwah, New Jersey

All rights reserved. No part of this book may be used
or reproduced in any manner whatsoever without written
permission from the publisher.

Printed in the United States of America
10   9   8   7   6   5   4   3

If you could be an animal,
which one would you like to be?

Perhaps you'd like to be a lion, prowling through the jungle. Or a bear, curled safely in its den. Or a bird, flying through the air. Or a dolphin, swimming swiftly through the water.

Almost everyone has a favorite animal. There are many different kinds of animals in the world. And each one is fascinating in its own special way.

How big and how small?

Animals come in many different sizes. Some are large. Some are small. The largest animal in the world is the blue whale. It may be 100 feet (30 meters) in length. The smallest animals are so small that they cannot be seen, except under a microscope.

Some animals have many legs, and some have no legs. Some have wings, and some have flippers. Some have hair or fur, while others have feathers or scales.

Suppose you wanted to divide all the animals in the world into different groups. You might group them by where they live. Then all the land animals would be in one group, and all the water animals would be in another group. Or you might group them by what they eat. Animals that eat plants would be in one group, and animals that eat meat would be in another. You might even group them by putting wild animals in one group, and tame animals in another.

How do scientists group animals?

One way that scientists group animals is to put those with backbones in one group and those with no backbones in another. Animals with backbones are called *vertebrates*. Animals that do not have backbones are called *invertebrates*.

Worms do not have backbones. So worms are invertebrates. Ants and butterflies and clams and lobsters are also invertebrates. Is a jellyfish an invertebrate? Is an octopus? Jellyfish and octopuses do not have backbones, so they are invertebrates.

BACKBONE

All invertebrates are cold-blooded. This means their body temperatures change. When the air is cold, their temperatures drop. When the air is warm, their temperatures rise.

Goldfish are vertebrates. They have backbones. Frogs and snakes and robins and bears also have backbones. Reach behind you and feel the middle of your back. You should be able to feel your backbone. People have backbones, so they are vertebrates, too.

Some vertebrates are cold-blooded. Goldfish, frogs, and snakes are cold-blooded. Some vertebrates are warm-blooded. The body of a warm-blooded animal does not grow cold when the air is cold. Its temperature remains about the same all the time. Robins, bears, and people are warm-blooded.

Scientists who study animals divide vertebrates and invertebrates into many smaller groups of animals.

Groups of invertebrates

In one group of invertebrates are the worms. In another group are the soft-bodied animals with shells. In another group are all the six-legged animals called insects. In another are all the eight-legged animals called spiders.

DON'T BUG ME!

Groups of vertebrates

The main groups of vertebrate animals are fish, amphibians, reptiles, birds, and mammals. Let's take a closer look at each of these groups of animals with backbones.

A *fish* is a cold-blooded animal that lives its entire life in the water. It breathes through gills, and its body is usually covered with scales. Goldfish and tunas and flounders are fish.

An *amphibian* is a cold-blooded animal that lives part of its life in the water and part of its life on land. When it lives in the water, it breathes through gills. When it comes out onto the land to live, it breathes with lungs. Frogs and toads and salamanders are amphibians.

A *reptile* is a cold-blooded animal that breathes through lungs. Snakes and turtles and lizards and crocodiles are reptiles. Reptiles have dry, scaly skin.

A warm-blooded animal that breathes through lungs and that has feathers on its body is called a *bird*. Robins and eagles and owls are birds that can fly. Penguins and ostriches are birds that cannot fly.

A warm-blooded animal that breathes through lungs and that has hair or fur on its body is called a *mammal*. Mammals feed their young with milk. Dogs and cats and bears and people are mammals.

Is a whale a fish or a mammal?

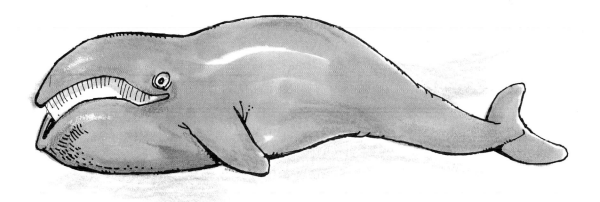

A whale looks like a fish, but it is really a mammal. It is warm-blooded. Blubber, or fat, helps keep it warm—even in icy waters. A whale breathes air through lungs. It would drown if it could not come up to the surface to breathe. A whale even has hair—but only a little. It has a few bristles of hair on its head. Like most other mammals, whales give birth to live babies, rather than by laying eggs. A baby whale is called a calf.

Baby animals

Many kinds of baby animals have names that are different from those of their parents. Baby bears and baby lions are called cubs. Baby horses and baby donkeys are called foals. Did you know that baby goats and baby antelopes are called kids? A baby goose is a gosling. A baby swan is a cygnet. A baby deer is a fawn. And a baby kangaroo is a joey.

All these baby animals look very much like their parents when they first come into the world. But some baby animals look very different from their parents. Do you know what baby butterflies and moths look like? Do you know what they are called?

Baby butterflies and baby moths are called caterpillars. They feed on the leaves of plants. Later, each caterpillar goes into a deep sleep inside a hard shell called a *chrysalis,* or inside a silken *cocoon.* When it awakens, it comes out of its chrysalis or cocoon as a butterfly or moth.

Baby frogs and baby toads also look very different from their parents. They are called tadpoles or polliwogs, and they look more like fish than frogs or toads. Frogs, toads, butterflies, and moths are some of the animals that change completely as they grow from babies to adults. This complete change of form is called *metamorphosis.*

EGGS

TADPOLE

FROG

Another way that scientists sometimes group animals depends on when the animals are active and when they sleep. Many animals sleep at night. But some sleep during the day and are active at night.

At night, while you are sound asleep, the animals that were sleeping during the day are wide awake. They are looking for something to eat. These are called *nocturnal* animals, or animals of the night. Owls and bats and raccoons are animals of the night. Many crickets, frogs, and turtles are also nocturnal animals.

What is migration?

When winter approaches, and the northern weather turns colder, many animals go south. This sort of trip is called *migration.* Each fall, robins and bluebirds migrate to the south. They migrate because food is hard to find during the northern winter, when everything is frozen or covered with snow. In warmer lands, they can find plenty of worms and insects to eat. In the spring, bluebirds and robins migrate north again.

Other animals also migrate. The orange-and-black monarch butterfly flies south each fall—to Mexico and California. Each spring, it returns north. Whales migrate from one part of the ocean to another. In the summer, they move toward colder water, where food is more plentiful. In the winter, they return to warmer waters, where they breed.

Salmon make long migrations from salt water to fresh water. When it is time to breed, they leave the ocean, where they have lived for years, and swim up into the rivers. After they reach their breeding grounds in shallow streams, they lay their eggs. Then they die. But the eggs hatch, and the young salmon swim down the river and into the sea.

The longest migration is made by a bird called the Arctic tern. In August, it leaves its nesting grounds on islands in the Arctic Ocean. It flies south for about 11,000 miles (17,700 kilometers), until it reaches Antarctica. Later, the birds begin the return trip north.

What is hibernation?

Some animals do not migrate when the weather turns cold. As snow powders the land and ice covers the lakes, they go into a deep sleep. This deep sleep lasts for several months. It is called *hibernation*. It is very hard to wake up an animal that is hibernating.

When an animal hibernates, its body temperature drops, and its heart begins to beat more slowly. Bats, ground squirrels, and hamsters hibernate. So do frogs and some fish. Bears sleep a lot during the winter, but they do not really hibernate. It is not hard to wake a sleeping bear in the winter—but if you are smart, you will let it sleep!

20

Are humans different than other animals?

Human beings are more intelligent than any other kind of animal. They are best able to solve problems and learn from experience. The next most intelligent animals are monkeys and apes. Dolphins are the most intelligent animals in the ocean. Pigs are the smartest animals with hoofs. Of the animals that gnaw, squirrels are the most intelligent. Then come birds, amphibians and reptiles, and fish. Animals that have no backbones are the least intelligent of all.

ENVIRONMENT
OR NOT, I'M
FREEZING!

Where do animals live?

Animals live in almost every area of the world. The kinds of animals that live in a particular area are the ones that are best suited to those surroundings. An animal's surroundings are called its *environment*.

Animals live in the mountains, in the grasslands, and in the forests. They live in steamy jungles, in scorching deserts, and in the frozen polar regions. They live on every continent and in every ocean in the world.

What kinds of animals live in the oceans?

In the ocean, there are fish of all shapes and all sizes. Some are flat, like flounders and halibut. Others are streamlined, like sharks and tuna. Some live in shallow water, and some live in the deep, dark parts of the ocean.

But fish are not the only animals that live in the sea. There are reptiles, like sea turtles and salt-water crocodiles. There are mammals, like whales and dolphins. And there are many invertebrate animals—sponges and jellyfish, starfish and sea cucumbers, snails and clams, lobsters and octopuses.

What animals live in the mountains?

If you went to the mountains, you might see a mountain goat or a bighorn sheep or even a mountain lion. But high in the highest mountains, you would probably see only insects and spiders.

What animals live at the North and South Poles?

Even in the deep freeze near the North Pole, there are animals. Polar bears and Alaskan brown bears feed on fish. Reindeer scratch at the snow, searching for plants that may be hidden underneath. Snowy owls and arctic hares and furry ermines blend in with the color of their environment. Fewer animals live near the South Pole. The best known is the penguin—a bird that cannot fly. It uses its wings as flippers when it swims through the icy water.

What animals live in the forests?

In the forests, you might see bears or foxes, moose or deer. Chipmunks and squirrels scamper about, gathering food for the winter. Raccoons and skunks also live in the forests, and so do muskrats and beavers. When the porcupine wanders through the woods, other animals usually stay away!

What animals live in the jungle?

In the jungles, or tropical forests, you can see armies of ants and long-tongued anteaters. In the trees are birds of every color and monkeys of every description. Tigers and other big cats silently stalk their prey, while huge snakes slither along the branches of the trees.

What animals live in the desert?

In the deserts, lizards and small snakes sun themselves on the rocks. But many of the animals that live in hot desert environments usually come out at night, when it is cooler. Then bats fly from their caves and snap up flying insects. Kangaroo rats and pocket mice leap about, searching for food. Coyotes and kit foxes are on the prowl, hunting for a tasty meal.

What animals live in the grasslands?

In the grasslands of Africa, there are lions and zebras, giraffes, elephants, and ostriches. The ostrich is the biggest bird in the world. If you stood next to an ostrich, you would have to look *up* to see its head! The giraffe is the tallest animal. Its long neck helps it reach the tender leaves near the tops of the trees. The elephant is the largest land animal. But the lion is the "king." When a lion roars, the sound can be heard from far away.

Do animals communicate?

Many animals communicate by making sounds. Birds sing to show the boundaries of their territory, or home area. Dogs bark and growl to warn others. When a gull finds food, it cries out loudly. Dolphins and whales "talk" by making high-pitched sounds.

Many animals communicate without sounds. When a bee finds food, it returns to the hive and "dances" in a special way. The dance tells other bees where the food is. A cat warns other animals away by raising the hair on its back and neck. A dog that feels friendly wags its tail. A firefly lights up to attacts other fireflies. A female moth gives off a special odor to attract male moths. A skunk can give off a very unpleasant odor to discourage its enemies from attacking.

Can you recognize these tracks?

Many animals leave "messages" that let you know they have been around. They leave *tracks*, or footprints in the soft ground or in the snow. Here are ten animal tracks you can learn to recognize.

Dog

Cat

Deer

Rabbit

Horse

Gull

Skunk

Opossum

Beaver

Raccoon

It's fun to study animals.

It's fun to learn about animals, to study their behavior, and to find out about their environments. The next time you hear the sound or the song of an animal, or see a set of animal tracks, try to guess what kind of animal it is.

Is it a vertebrate or an invertebrate? Is it a meat-eater or a plant-eater? Is it tame or wild? Is it cold-blooded or warm-blooded? Does it hibernate? Does it migrate? How does it communicate? How intelligent is it?

The answers to these questions may be surprising. They will surely be interesting, for animals are a fascinating part of the world in which we live.